A TRUE BOOK™

Why It Matters
The
U.S. Constitution

Moira Rose Donohue

Children's Press®
An Imprint of Scholastic Inc.

Content Consultant
Kerry Sautner
Chief Learning Officer
National Constitution Center
Philadelphia, Pennsylvania

We thank the staff of the National Constitution Center in
Philadelphia, Pennsylvania, for their help with this book.

Teacher Adviser
Rachel Hsieh

Library of Congress Cataloging-in-Publication Data
Names: Donohue, Moira Rose, author.
Title: The U.S. Constitution : why it matters to you / Moira Rose Donohue.
Other titles: US Constitution
Description: New York, NY : Children's Press, an imprint of Scholastic, Inc., 2020. | Series: A true book |
    Includes bibliographical references and index.
Identifiers: LCCN 2019007685 | ISBN 9780531231838 (library binding : alk. paper) | ISBN 9780531239957
    (pbk. : alk. paper)
Subjects: LCSH: United States. Constitution--Juvenile literature. | Constitutional history--United States--
    Juvenile literature.
Classification: LCC E303 .D66 2020 | DDC 342.7302/9--dc23
LC record available at https://lccn.loc.gov/2019007685

All rights reserved. Published in 2020 by Children's Press, an imprint of Scholastic Inc.
Printed in North Mankato, MN, USA 113

SCHOLASTIC, CHILDREN'S PRESS, A TRUE BOOK™, and associated logos are trademarks and/or
registered trademarks of Scholastic Inc.

Scholastic Inc., 557 Broadway, New York, NY 10012

1 2 3 4 5 6 7 8 9 10 R 29 28 27 26 25 24 23 22 21 20

**Front cover: A copy of the
Constitution on the U.S. flag**

**Back cover: A family viewing the Constitution
at the National Archives in Washington, D.C.**

Find the Truth!

Everything you are about to read is true *except* for one of the sentences on this page.

Which one is **TRUE**?

T or F   George Washington wrote the U.S. Constitution by himself.

T or F   The Constitution set up three branches of government.

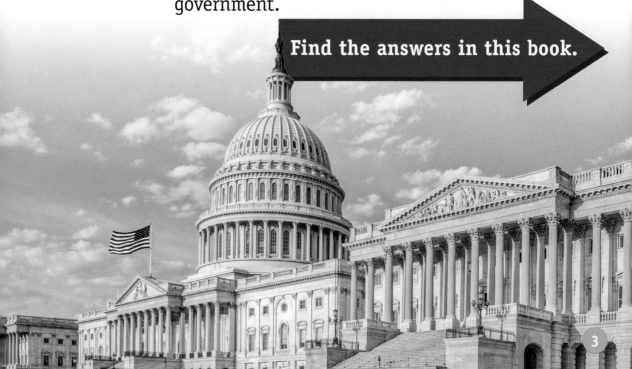

Find the answers in this book.

3

Contents

The **BIG** Truth

Learning About the Government

We the People

The U.S. Constitution is the law of the land for the entire country.

Students march in Washington, D.C., to protest school shootings.

Colonial soldiers

5

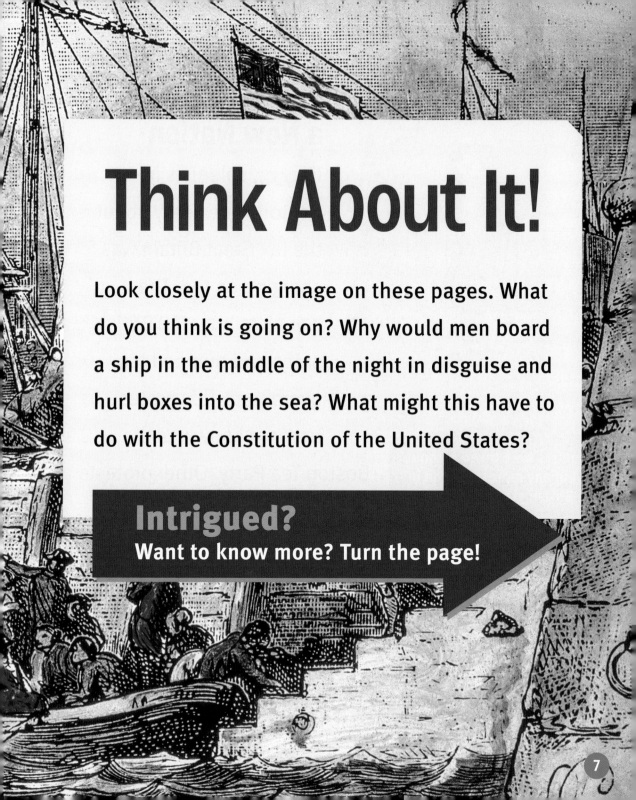

Think About It!

Look closely at the image on these pages. What do you think is going on? Why would men board a ship in the middle of the night in disguise and hurl boxes into the sea? What might this have to do with the Constitution of the United States?

Intrigued?
Want to know more? Turn the page!

Nothing was thought of but this taxation, and the easiest method of liquidation.

T-A-X

'Twas enough to vex the souls of the men of Boston Town, to read this under the seal of the Crown.

TAX· ON· TEA· 3d per lb

They were loyal subjects of George the Third; so they believed and so they averred, but this bristling, offensive placard set on the walls, was worse than a bayonet.

Colonists were taxed without having any representation in the British government.

Building a New Nation

In 1773, colonists in Boston were angry about the tax Great Britain was charging on tea. The colonists boarded British ships and dumped tea overboard. This protest became known as the Boston Tea Party. Other protests followed. Two years later, the colonists began fighting the Revolutionary War (1775–1783). During the war, the colonies passed a set of rules called the Articles of Confederation. After the war ended, the states still tried to follow these rules, but they did not work well for the new nation.

The United States needed to make changes to support a successful nation. Yet what would those changes be? How would the states work together? Who would make decisions? How would the government work with and for everyone living in the nation? State representatives decided to meet and debate these and many other questions. Their discussion would end with a new document—the U.S. Constitution.

Today, you can see the original Constitution at the National Archives Museum in Washington, D.C.

The Constitution is more than 200 years old. The original document was only four pages long.

Thanks to James Madison, we know what was discussed during the convention. He sat in the front row and scribbled down what people said.

The delegates signed the Constitution on September 17, 1787.

A Moment in History

On February 21, 1787, state leaders agreed to hold a meeting, called a convention, to fix the Articles of Confederation. Fifty-five **delegates** representing 12 states traveled to Philadelphia in May. These delegates became known as the framers of the Constitution. James Madison from Virginia arrived early. Many other delegates were late! Rhode Island did not send any delegates at all.

A New Document

Once the meeting started, the delegates elected George Washington as president of the convention. The delegates quickly realized that they needed to replace the Articles of Confederation with a brand-new document. Starting from scratch would require a lot of thought. Luckily, Madison and other delegates had planned ahead, creating an outline for a new government.

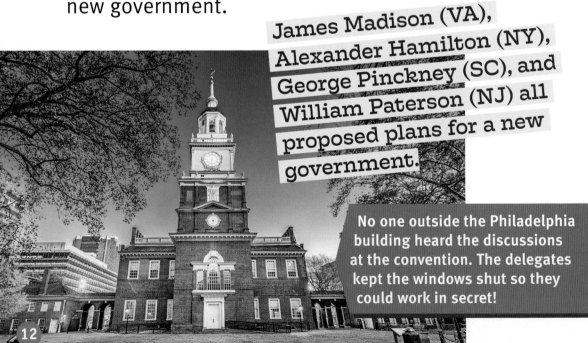

James Madison (VA), Alexander Hamilton (NY), George Pinckney (SC), and William Paterson (NJ) all proposed plans for a new government.

No one outside the Philadelphia building heard the discussions at the convention. The delegates kept the windows shut so they could work in secret!

"Do we want a democracy where every vote counts or where we count every vote?"

Wording is important when writing laws. Lawmakers are careful to write so that people will understand a law's meaning. What are the lawmakers in this cartoon debating? How might the two different phrases be interpreted differently?

Three Branches

Madison's plan would create a strong, central democratic **republic**. Citizens in each state would elect representatives to the national government to make decisions. It would establish "a separation of powers" by setting up three branches of government. The legislative branch would make the laws. The executive branch would enforce the laws. The judicial branch would **interpret** the laws.

The Great Compromise

The plan wasn't perfect. One of the biggest issues was the lawmaking branch. Large states wanted the number of representatives to be based on population. This gave each citizen equal say in government. Small states disagreed. Places with larger populations would always outvote them! The Great Compromise created two different lawmaking houses. In one, every state would have two votes, giving each state equal say. In the other, representation would be based on population.

UNCLAIMED TERRITORY

RUPERT'S LAND (GREAT BRITAIN)

NEW HAMPSHIRE

VERMONT REPUBLIC

MASSACHUSETTS

NEW YORK

RHODE ISLAND
CONNECTICUT

NORTHWEST TERRITORY

PENNSYLVANIA

NEW JERSEY

DELAWARE

COLONY OF LOUISIANA (SPAIN)

MARYLAND

VIRGINIA

NEW SPAIN (SPAIN)

SOUTHWEST TERRITORY

NORTH CAROLINA

SOUTH CAROLINA

GEORGIA

FLORIDA (SPAIN)

○ U.S. state
○ U.S. territory
○ Disputed area
○ Other territories

This map shows which countries claimed or controlled parts of what is now the United States in 1790. This was three years after the Constitutional Convention.

The Issue of Slavery

Slavery is a brutal system that allows a person to own another person as property. Enslaved people have no rights and no control over their lives. In what became the United States, slavery began in 1619, and officially ended in 1865. However, some delegates fought to end it at the Constitutional Convention. Other delegates fought to keep it.

Slavery also sparked disagreement over how to determine the number of congresspeople each state should have. Many enslaved people lived in the South. If they were counted as part of each state's population, southern states would have more lawmakers—and more power. Delegates at the time decided to account for three-fifths of all enslaved people. The number was not based on any science or logic. It was just a way to end the argument temporarily.

Slaves working in cotton fields often had to work 15 or more hours a day.

We the People

After four months of debating, the delegates agreed to a new government. They did not include a list of individual rights in the Constitution. That would come later. Gouverneur Morris, a delegate from Pennsylvania, organized the Constitution into seven parts called articles. He began the document with, "We the people of the United States." This signaled that the new nation was united. Next, the document went to the states for **ratification**, or approval.

Timeline of Early American Government

The Continental Congress adopts the Articles of Confederation.

The Revolutionary War ends after about eight years of fighting.

1776

1777

1781

1783

The 13 American colonies declare independence from Great Britain.

ARTICLES
OF
CONFEDERATION
AND
PERPETUAL UNION
BETWEEN THE
STATES
OF

The final state ratifies the Articles of Confederation.

The Road to Ratification

Nine states needed to approve the Constitution, but not everyone liked the new document. For example, some people argued that the strong national government would reduce states' rights. In response, politicians Alexander Hamilton, James Madison, and John Jay wrote 85 essays in favor of the Constitution. Delaware became the first state to ratify the Constitution in December 1787. By 1788, enough states had ratified it, so it became law.

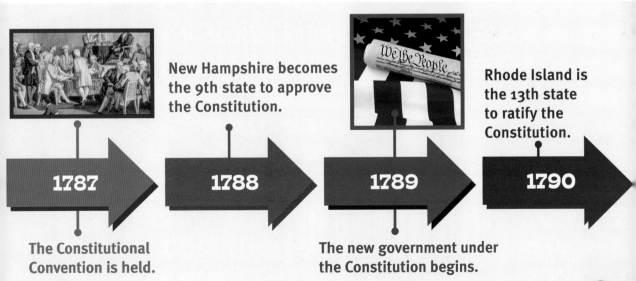

New Hampshire becomes the 9th state to approve the Constitution.

Rhode Island is the 13th state to ratify the Constitution.

1787

1788

1789

1790

The Constitutional Convention is held.

The new government under the Constitution begins.

The nation's capital was in New York City and then Philadelphia, Pennsylvania, before George Washington moved it to Washington, D.C.

Congress meets in the Capitol.

CHAPTER

2

Who Makes the Rules Here?

The delegates knew the country would need additional laws from time to time. This is why they created the legislative branch in the Constitution. Article I, the longest article of the Constitution, explains how Congress works. Remember the Great Compromise? That's how Congress came to have two houses: the Senate and the House of Representatives. Both houses must agree before a **bill** becomes a law.

The Senate

Each state elects two senators. That gives the small states an equal say in the Senate. Senators are elected for six-year terms. The vice president oversees meetings of the Senate but can only vote in case of a tie.

To be a senator, you have to wait until you're 30 years old. But at 16, you can work in the Senate as a page. Pages are messengers and helpers appointed by senators.

Vice President Joe Biden (right) swears in Senator Kamala Harris of California.

Do you know who your representative is?

Bryan Steil of Wisconsin celebrates being elected to a seat in the House of Representatives.

The House of Representatives

The number of representatives who sit in the House of Representatives is based on a state's population. Representatives serve two-year terms. They must be 25 years old. Members of the House elect a speaker to be in charge.

The original Constitution provided one representative for every 30,000 people. In 1929, Congress limited the number of representatives to 435. Today, a member of the House represents about 750,000 people.

There Ought to Be a Law

Article I also lists Congress's powers, such as coining money, declaring war, and of course making laws!

To make or change a law, a member of Congress introduces a bill. A committee holds hearings about it. Then the house that introduced the bill votes on it. If it passes, it goes to the other house for a vote. If you think we need a new law, write to your representative or senator about it.

Not So Fast!

When the delegates wrote the Constitution, they decided to create a system of checks and balances to keep any branch from becoming too powerful. It "checks" the power of each branch to keep the government "balanced." For example, Congress writes and passes bills. But the president must sign a bill before it becomes a law. The president can also choose to veto, or reject, it. Then the bill goes back to Congress, which can vote to overrule the president. If a law doesn't follow the Constitution, the highest court in the judicial branch can get rid of the law.

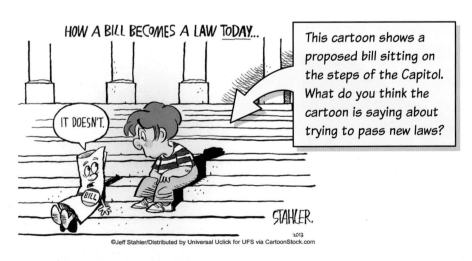

HOW A BILL BECOMES A LAW TODAY...

IT DOESN'T.

BILL

STAHLER.

2013

©Jeff Stahler/Distributed by Universal Uclick for UFS via CartoonStock.com

This cartoon shows a proposed bill sitting on the steps of the Capitol. What do you think the cartoon is saying about trying to pass new laws?

Learning About the Government

Civics is the study of the rights and responsibilities we have as citizens. Civics programs in schools help explain the role that people can have in the government through actions such as voting and paying taxes. Most states require students to spend time learning about civics. In other states, schools don't have to cover the subject at all.

What do you think?

Should schools require students to study civics?

YES	NO
✔ It creates voters who are better informed.	✔ It takes time and energy away from other important subjects, such as math and reading.
✔ It makes people more likely to participate in the government, whether as a member of the public or as an elected official.	✔ Some states require students to pass the Citizenship Test, which new U.S. residents must pass to become citizens, before they can graduate. This can make it harder for some students to graduate.
✔ It builds trust between the public and government leaders.	✔ Some of the civics programs that exist are not very effective. The programs should be improved before they are required.
✔ It helps people become better at holding elected officials accountable.	✔ Civics information can be worked into other subjects, such as history.

The president is the commander in chief, or highest leader, of the U.S. military.

President Donald Trump speaks to members of the military.

Take Me to Your Leader!

Article II of the Constitution sets up the executive branch, which executes, or carries out, laws. The delegates at the Constitutional Convention feared giving too much executive power to one person, as Great Britain had with its king. They considered having three people in charge. But after days of debate, they decided on a single elected leader: the president. The president commands the armed forces and defines the country's goals and plans. Can you name our current president?

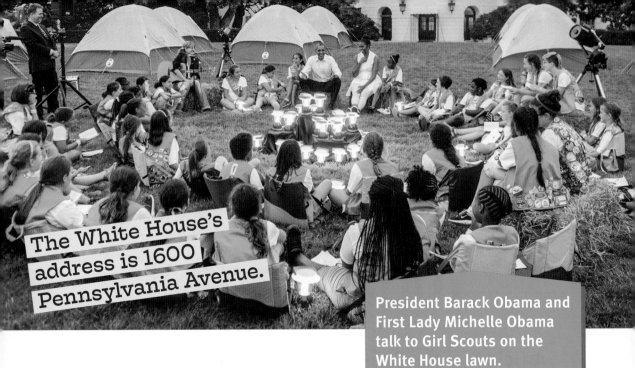

The White House's address is 1600 Pennsylvania Avenue.

President Barack Obama and First Lady Michelle Obama talk to Girl Scouts on the White House lawn.

Becoming President

Do you want to be president? Article II of the Constitution says you must be a natural-born citizen, have lived in the United States for 14 years or more, and be at least 35 years old.

The president serves a four-year term. The original Constitution didn't limit the number of times a president could be reelected. But the 22nd **Amendment**, passed in 1947, limited the president to two terms.

The College That Isn't a College

Should people vote directly for the president? The framers did not think so, so they created the Electoral College. Under Article II, people vote for a presidential **candidate**. But they're actually voting for an **elector** in that candidate's political party.

In most states, all the electors must vote for the person who wins the popular vote in the state. Sometimes a candidate gets the most votes in the nation but doesn't win in enough states to become president!

This cartoon is making fun of how people were chosen to rule in England by referring to the legend of King Arthur. How does the U.S. Constitution say a president should be chosen?

"You pulled a sword out of a stone and they made you king? Is that *constitutional*?"

Impeachment proceedings begin for President Bill Clinton inside the Senate chamber in 1999.

Nº 15

106TH CONGRESS—FIRST SESSION
United States Senate

Impeachment Trial of the
PRESIDENT OF THE UNITED STATES

Sergeant at Arms United States Senate

ADMIT BEARER TO THE SENATE FAMILY GALLERY

Impeachment

Do you think the president should ever be fired? The framers thought so. Under Article II, the president and other officials can be removed if they are found guilty of **treason** or other crimes. The process begins with the House of Representatives voting to **impeach** the official. Then the Senate turns itself into a court. It tries the case, with the chief justice of the Supreme Court in charge.

Parkland

The office of the president serves all the people of the United States, including students. On February 14, 2018, a gunman entered Marjory Stoneman Douglas High School in Parkland, Florida, and killed 17 people. Students were heartbroken. They were also angry and frustrated. This was one of many school shootings that had occurred over the years. The Parkland students took a stand and demanded more gun control. They organized marches and met with Florida's governor. They also spoke with the president to share their opinions and perspectives.

Hundreds of thousands of people demonstrate in Washington, D.C., for stronger gun control.

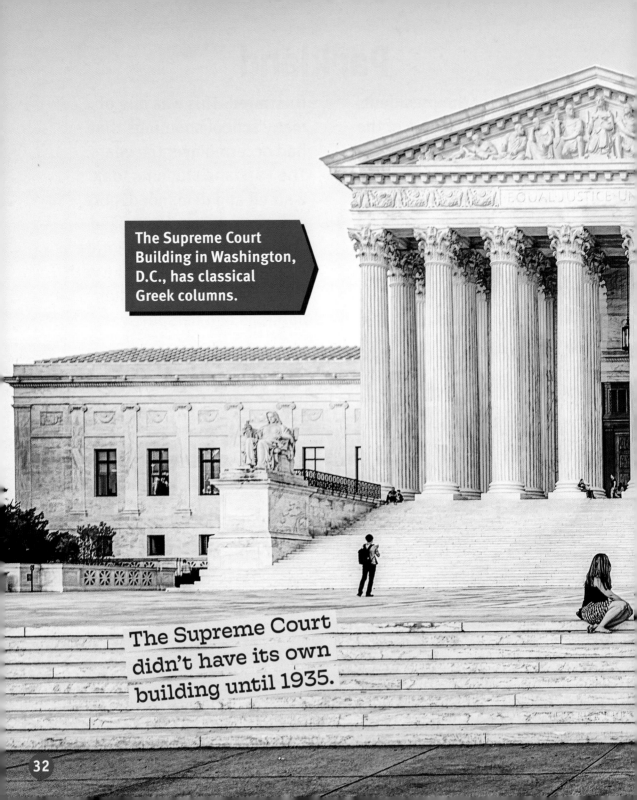

The Supreme Court Building in Washington, D.C., has classical Greek columns.

The Supreme Court didn't have its own building until 1935.

Nine Wise People

The framers wanted to make sure the ideas of the Constitution were followed. Article III sets up a judicial system to review and interpret the law, with the Supreme Court as the highest court in the land.

Congress sets the number of justices. They serve for life so they won't be swayed by political changes. The first court consisted of six white men. What do you notice about the nine justices who sit on the Supreme Court today?

Supreme Court justices

The System

Today, people file 7,000 to 8,000 cases a year with the Supreme Court. The court can hear only about 80 of those, so it chooses cases that raise important issues. Article III gives Congress the power to set up additional federal courts to handle other cases.

In an important case in 1803, *Marbury v. Madison*, the Supreme Court established the idea of judicial review. This put the Supreme Court in charge of deciding if a law was constitutional, or followed the Constitution.

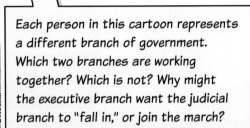

Each person in this cartoon represents a different branch of government. Which two branches are working together? Which is not? Why might the executive branch want the judicial branch to "fall in," or join the march?

Landmark Cases

Sometimes the Supreme Court overrules itself. In *Plessy v. Ferguson* (1896), the court decided that "separate but equal" schools for black and white children were permitted under the Constitution. This later changed with the decision *Brown v. Board of Education* (1954). The justices said "separate but equal" was unconstitutional.

Thurgood Marshall (center) argued *Brown v. Board of Education* before the Supreme Court and later became a justice himself.

Recently, the court decided cases on presidential elections, free speech, and immigration. Can you think of some ways these cases may have affected you?

The U.S. Constitution is the world's oldest written constitution in use today.

The Constitution applies to everyone!

Other Articles and Amendments

The Constitution has four more articles. Article IV describes how states interact with one another, the federal government, and residents of other states. It establishes the United States as a single, connected nation. Article V is where the framers allow for change. It outlines the process for amending the Constitution. Article VI says the Constitution is the supreme law of the land. And Article VII describes how the states must ratify the Constitution.

The Bill of Rights

The ink on the Constitution was barely dry before Congress amended it. Some people worried that the Constitution didn't protect basic freedoms. So in 1789, Congress approved 12 amendments that went to the states for ratification. By 1791, the states had ratified 10 of them. These 10 are now called the Bill of Rights. They include protections such as the right to a fair trial and the freedoms of speech, religion, and the press.

The 1st Amendment in the Bill of Rights gives us freedom of speech. It protects our right to hold demonstrations.

The democratic principles of the Iroquois Constitution greatly influenced the U.S. Constitution.

The 13th Amendment freed all victims of slavery in the United States.

Other Important Amendments

After the Civil War, Congress passed three amendments to protect victims of slavery. The 13th Amendment, passed in 1865, outlawed slavery. The 14th gave all citizens equal protection under the law. The 15th gave male citizens the right to vote, regardless of race.

The 14th and 15th amendments did not apply to Native Americans until the 20th century. The Constitution originally stated that Native Americans were not citizens, though they had lived on the land thousands of years before the colonists took it from them. In 1924, the Indian Citizenship Act granted Native Americans U.S. citizenship.

New York City kids celebrate the anniversary of the 24th Amendment.

Expanding Voting Rights

In 1787, only white men who owned property or were wealthy could vote. It took laws, protests, and other actions to change this. Here are some constitutional amendments that expanded voting rights:

★ 15th Amendment (1870) gave male citizens the right to vote, regardless of race

★ 19th Amendment (1920) gave all women the right to vote

★ 24th Amendment (1964) banned federal poll taxes, which kept many poor people from voting

★ 26th Amendment (1971) lowered the voting age from 21 to 18

Even with these amendments, there have been obstacles for voters. At times, some voters had to pay a local tax or pass a test. Many people argue that citizens can still face challenges registering to vote or casting their votes.

You can honor the Constitution's idea of a citizen-led government by standing up for everyone's right to vote. And when you're old enough, vote in every election. Our government works best when everyone takes part!

This cartoon shows the Constitution reading a book about bullies. Why would the document want to read this kind of book? Who might "bully" the Constitution, and why?

Climate Change

Kids can tackle issues that can affect their future long before they are even able to vote.

You don't have to wait until you're an adult to file a lawsuit. Since 2010, a nonprofit group has been helping young people around the country sue federal and state governments. The children want environmental protection laws. They believe that they will not be able to enjoy this country in the future if climate change isn't addressed.

Levi Draheim announces the lawsuit he and other students filed against the state of Florida.

These plaintiffs, or people who bring a case against someone in court, are trying to protect beautiful Florida beaches like this one.

In 2018, eight children sued the Florida governor. They argued that the state's actions have hurt Florida's beaches and marine life. This puts the future health of the ecosystems in danger. According to the lawsuit, the damages deny the children their rights to life, liberty, and property which are mentioned in the Bill of Rights. Lawsuits like this are part of a larger movement that includes kids and adults. These activists are working to protect our planet and its wildlife for future generations.

Get Involved!

You may not be old enough to vote yet, but you can still let your voice be heard. Here are some tips on how you can do this:

Learn about the issues. Read, watch, or listen to the news from multiple sources.

Talk with adults about which candidates you support and why.

Hold a voter registration drive at your school.

Help out with a campaign by calling, writing, or texting voters for federal, state, and local elections.

Write to your representative or senator if you have an idea for a new law.

Did you find the truth?

F George Washington wrote the U.S. Constitution by himself.

T The Constitution set up three branches of government.

Resources

The book you just read is a first introduction to the U.S. Constitution, and to the history and government of our country. There is always more to learn and discover. In addition to this title, we encourage you to seek out complementary resources.

Other books in this series:

 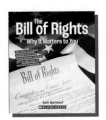 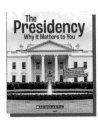 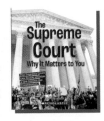 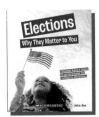

You can also look at:

Cheney, Lynne V., and Greg Harlin (illust.). *We the People: The Story of Our Constitution*. New York: Simon & Schuster Books for Young Readers, 2012.

Demuth, Patricia Brennan, and Tim Foley (illust.). *What Is the Constitution?* New York: Penguin Workshop, 2018.

Editors of Time for Kids (ed.). *Time for Kids: Our Nation's Documents*. New York: Time Inc. Books, 2018.

Paul, Caroline. *You Are Mighty: A Guide to Changing the World*. New York: Bloomsbury, Children's Books, 2018.

Glossary

amendment (uh-MEND-muhnt) a change that is made to a law or a legal document

bill (BIL) a written plan for a new law, to be debated and passed by a body of legislators

candidate (KAN-duh-date) a person who is applying for a job or running in an election

civics (SIV-iks) the study of the way government works and of how to be a good citizen of a community or country

delegates (DEL-ih-guts) people who represent other people at a meeting or in a legislature

elector (ih-LEK-tur) a member of the Electoral College in the United States

impeach (im-PEECH) to bring formal charges against a public official for misconduct

interpret (in-TUR-prit) to figure out what something means

ratification (rat-uh-fih-KAY-shun) the action of agreeing or approving officially

republic (ri-PUHB-lik) a form of government in which the people have the power to elect representatives who manage the government

treason (TREE-zuhn) the crime of being disloyal to your country by spying for another country or by helping an enemy during a war

Index

Page numbers in **bold** indicate illustrations.

About the Author

Moira Rose Donohue majored in political science in college and studied the Constitution while in law school. She spent most of her 20-year career as a lawyer drafting federal legislation. She has seen the original Constitution at the National Archives Museum and keeps a copy on her bookshelf. The author of over 30 books for children, she lives in St. Petersburg, Florida, with her dog, Petunia.